Nature's Embrace

Book I

Hello Audrey!
It was great singing & serenading the dolphins with you & Charley in Hawaii —

By JoeBaby

thanks for helping 'PR' the book!
Love, JoeBaby

Nature's Embrace

©2001 JoeBaby and Joseph Michael Noonan

All rights reserved. Except as otherwise permitted by applicable law, and except for quotations in book reviews, no part of *Nature's Embrace* may be reproduced, stored, or transmitted in any form, or by any means—electronic, mechanical, or otherwise, including photocopy, recording, or any information storage and retrieval system—without permission in writing from Planetary Partners.

Sequoias photo–©1996 Barry Kaplan

Back cover photo by Judy Noonan

All other photos and graphics–©2001 JoeBaby

Cover and text design by Hird Graphic Design

Library of Congress Catalog Card Number: 00-93127

ISBN #0-9703698-0-8

Published by:
Planetary Partners
13 Pl. Is. Blvd.
Newbury, MA 01951
USA
(978) 499-4960

Printed in Canada

Table of Contents

Acknowledgements

Welcome!

Empty Space

Dedication

Part 1 – Elemental Adventures

Flower Rub Reverie 21
Bahamian Watsu 33
Eyes of the Beholder 43
Winter's Call 51
Baby Beach Buddha 57

Part 2 – Poetry & Praise

Late Night Storm 67
Somewhere Among the Flowers 71
Sledding 77
Drunk Again! 81

Part 3 – Body Wisdom

Nipples 87
Wolfish Friend 97
Sequoias to the Rescue 107
Chills & Thrills 115
Dolphin Matriarch 121

Conclusion

Thanks! 132
Planetary Partners 133
About JoeBaby 135
Recommended Reading 136

Acknowledgements

Thanks to my beautiful wife Najda Maria for helping bring the Divine to life in our partnership and in our home. Thanks for seeing my sacredness when I can't. Thanks for your wonderful, ongoing support of this book. And thanks for encouraging my connection with Nature.

Thanks to my son Mark for showing me how much love there is to being a parent. Thanks for your joyous spirit, for reminding me how to drop everything for the moment of Now, for being a boy who loves to sing, dance, run and wrestle. Thanks for being in my family.

Thank you Gurumayi for showing me the nectar of chanting, Gangaji for the clarity of your message and Guadeloupe for your protection. Thanks Karunamayi for your love and your encouragement of this book. Thank you Divine Mother for the love, inspiration and gentleness you bring me.

Thank you Bob Noonan for all the writing tips and the great editing. And thank you Bob White for your awesome support and encouragement with this book, for your masterful coaching, and for seeing the greatness in those around you.

Thank you Debbie Hird for helping turn this stack of papers into a work of art. Thanks Mike Gazzola for guiding me through the printing process. Thanks to the Mastermind Alliance, to Joe Gerry, Jane Gibbs, Sarah Nevin, Rich Faler, Judy Noonan, Barry Kaplan, Silke Fuchshofen, E. Gene Chambers, Dan Mahoney and all the people on the Planetary Partner's e-mail list for your support.

Thank you Elements, Devas, Pan and all beings of Light, for the beauty you create, pointing us back again to our true nature.

Thanks to everyone who said "Yes!" along the way.

(The unabridged Appreciations page is on the Planetary Partner's website at www.PlanetaryPartners.com)

Welcome

Once upon a time, I was a child immersed in a world of magic and awe. Life was a blast—all the plants, trees and animals around me were my friends. I'd jump out of bed every morning, ready and eager for the day's adventures.

You know the story. As I got older, I learned how important it was to look good. And being playful definitely didn't look good. So I put aside my 'childish' nature, hid my love of games, of flowers, of talking with the wind and trees. Just as my own son at the tender age of six asked me not to hug him in front of the school bus, so I in my own youth hid my joys and affections.

I took my cues from the men around me. I acted tough, walked stiff as a board, learned to look aloof and uncaring. I began to mistrust and fear my feelings, afraid they'd pop out and shame me, like the time in 4th grade when I lost a fight with the new kid in town. I didn't shed a tear until I got home and my older brother asked me what was wrong. Shame burned hot in my face as tears and sobs exploded from me. Damn, I just wasn't tough enough. Not yet.

From what I could see, it was the route of all boys. We modeled war heroes and stuffed everything else. We learned that to dominate was the goal. Life was a pecking order of superiority. Over time, I forgot my love of nature and the joy it brought me.

I studied hard and learned that science had an explanation for everything. I lived in a flux of electrons that were empty and without life. The cool rush of the wind was a bunch of hot air molecules hurrying to meet a bunch of cold air molecules somewhere else. Nature, once the caretaker of my own soul, became a chemical reaction we manipulate to serve our will.

It was a world view that left me empty. I was rich in knowledge, but dry in spirit. My heart was heavy. And so I searched, as we all have, down different paths in pursuit of something meaningful. I learned many great practices, tools to bring peace, happiness, fame and fortune. As Gangaji would say, they were all strategies, ways to chase pleasure and avoid pain, the pain of my own broken heart.

And always, unknowingly, when I was at wit's end, when I was dry and empty, it was to nature I'd go. It was in the woods, the hills and the meadows I'd collapse, abandoning my struggles. Here I'd find the peace I so desperately sought.

Slowly, over time, I've pulled together the pieces of my childhood. Like an old treasure map, I've followed it to the buried treasure; the beauty and simplicity of my youth.

For me, it's simple. When I'm outdoors, I'm in my lover's arms. Through the presence of the sun, water, earth and wind, I feel the greatness of our creation. Here I'm alive, vibrantly and vitally part of the whole.

To stay here, I've had to confront the bogeymen of my past, the guardians I put in place to make sure I'd never return. It's taken me awhile, because to build a life of directness to what I love, I've had to face these fears, feel them moving within me. And while I turned it into a lot of struggle, truly, I had no choice. It was a matter of life or death.

Thankfully, gratefully, through this willingness, I've found an incredible grace. Nature never left. She's right here, ever present, ever ready. I'm once again completely blown away by the incredible beauty of flowers, smile with joy from the warm kiss of the sun.

These stories tell of my journey back to life. They share how my understanding of self, of the world and of the Divine has been shaken, rattled, reborn.

It brings me great joy to share this book with you. Just as a well aimed breeze blows away the dead ash from smoldering coals, bringing forth fresh fire and flame, the Divine in her many ways has re-ignited the fire within my own heart. It is my wish that these stories help do the same for you.

Bon Voyage!

Joe Baby

Empty Space

"There's more to life than increasing its speed"

Mahatma Gandhi

There's a lot of empty space in this book. It's by design. We lead such busy lives; going, going, going, sometimes days go by without a break.

Cows have four stomachs. How cool. They seem so content, laying out in the field, looking mindlessly around, chewing their cud. They're giving their food time to digest, savoring it fully.

This is what happens to me in nature. I slow down, pause, slip the mind into neutral and coast. It's in the coasting I find the magic, it's here I feel the Divine's embrace.

The empty space in this book's an invitation to you to pause, to reflect, to savor and digest. It's an opportunity for the vastness of our oneness to reveal itself again.

Dedication

To the Divine Mother,

Gaia, the Goddess,

the Feminine spirit within

that nourishes and sustains all life ~

To the Four Elements;

Fire, Earth, Air & Water,

through whom you reach out and touch us

With great joy and gratitude

I dedicate this book to you

in all your many forms

Jai Devi!

Part 1

Elemental Adventures

*"I am made to love the pond and meadow
as the wind is made to ripple the water"*

Thoreau

Flower Rub Reverie

It was a beautiful spring day. The sun was out and shining. I was in a T-shirt and shorts, headed for the island on the marsh.

I drove down the crumbling tar road, right up to the gate. This was once the driveway of an old farm-house, the only occupant of this marsh island. It's long since been bulldozed, the land turned into a wildlife refuge.

I park my car and hop the rusty metal gate, landing on the old wooden bridge. I see the incoming tide, hear its loud rush of water beneath me.

The water's pushing, pushing to get past the narrow throat of the bridge. Low tide's tiny trickle has returned, become a huge force of seawater eager to get upstream. It's alive, a great big flush of saline rushing to soak itself in the thousands of acres of salt marsh, thirsty and dry after hours without a drink.

This bridge is a threshold for me, the magic wardrobe in a C. S. Lewis novel. It's where I enter a land as old as time itself. I pause here, to say a blessing, acknowledging the spirits of this place. Though they are mostly invisible to my eye, I want them to know I'm aware and appreciative of them.

My salutations done, I cross the last of the marsh, stepping over bits of driftwood and marsh hay left from the last high tide.

The road reaches the island, rises up. It's boarded on both sides by a broken row of old willow trees, thick twisted trunks standing guard. Some are dead, others dying, still others vitally alive. The ground's covered with their fallen limbs, many as thick as my thigh, torn off from winter storms.

These are massive trees, even the dead ones vibrate energy. They remind me of old wizards in ratty clothing. Some are covered with fresh shoots, new life popping out of nooks and crannies, like the salt and pepper hairs from old men's ears.

They barely notice me as I walk beneath them. I took it personal once, then came to see they were busy about their own work, long ago having lost interest in the fickle nature of man. I dare say you could cut one down and it wouldn't notice, so about their business they are. Their focused intensity to their alchemical tasks endears me to them.

I continue up the hill, senses on alert. All spring I've watched a procession of flowers bloom here, each visit brings a new wave of color. First there were crocuses, faint purples and yellows barely visible underfoot. Then there were daffodils, sharp bright whites and yellows poking out of last year's grass. Then came apple blossoms; white and pink, and the purple blossoms of an ornamental tree.

I reach the top, beneath another canopy of willows, this a younger grove with crowns intact. Just past them I see a flash of purple. My heart jumps.

They're in bloom! A huge patch of lilacs, gone bush wild since the end of pruning decades ago. A wild and wooly bunch, spilling over onto what's left of the road. I walk towards them slowly, my chest swelling.

I remember the lilacs of my childhood, purple and white flowers blooming in our back yard and on the road to school. I remember their smell, and the feeling of abundance they gave me. I used to pick them, bring them indoors for the jar on the kitchen table.

I loved lilacs then and I love them still. They're so vibrant and alive, heralding spring with great vitality and recklessness. There's no holding back with lilacs, they give themselves fully to the world.

Suddenly I smell their thick sweet scent. It makes me dizzy, pulls me from the past to here, to them. My heart beats faster, and my step quickens.

I get closer, hear the steady humming of bees. A few more steps and I see them, flying thick among the flowers. There must be hundreds. Honey bees, bumble bees, small emerald green bees, bees of all kinds. They look like a horde of leprechauns standing three deep at the bar, laughing and jesting with raised mugs, quaffing an elemental thirst.

The flowers are at their peak. Each branch is loaded with blossoms, many are drooping to the ground. I make my own beeline for the thickest part, burying my head in one bunch after another. I sniff and sniff and sniff.

Time passes. I don't know how much, nor do I care.

I'm a kid in a candy store, the owner throwing the counter wide open and saying go ahead, help yourself. I stuff myself, breathing in their fragrance over and over again. I'm dizzy, my head swooning. God it feels good.

Every now and then I feel an urge to move on. "Okay, that's enough, let's go." What's the hurry, I wonder, and bury my head again. After another round, in the lull between reveries, the voice returns. "Okay, that's good. Time to get going."

I stop and close my eyes. I see an image of myself, a teenager with a man's features, impatiently tapping

his foot, glancing between me and his watch. He's
tired of waiting. "Let's go," he demands, the air of
authority thick in his voice. He reminds me of my dad.

Suddenly I'm a ten year old being chastised. I feel
foolish, want to hide my head, look away. He's got
things to do, and I'm holding him up. I feel bad for
my love of flowers, it's keeping him from more
important things.

I see it all so clearly, my ghosts from the past. He
wanted to usher me away from the things I loved and
on to the things the world demands of grown men. I
feel compassion for him, know the emptiness of his
labors. Right now smelling these flowers is the most
important thing in the world. I bless him, wish him
well, and turn back to my flowers.

They're right here, ready and waiting. I dive back in.
The more I enjoy them, the more they give. The
more they give, the more I crave. I feel like a salt
marsh that's been bone dry and thirsty for eons,
lapping up every drop.

They encourage this ravenous thirst, saying, "Yes,
drink deeply. It pleases us to be enjoyed so." My

desire, my appetite, my hunger grows, becomes a huge hungry maw, wide enough for the whole lilac bush, itself the size of a house.

The vastness of this hunger surprises me. It's huge– way beyond my own. It overshadows me, eager to taste the flower's offering. At first I'm startled, over- whelmed by so great a thirst, but soon I surrender, and am awash in a flow of nectar. No longer a man among flowers, I'm humanity imbibing the divine.

I drink the essence of all the lilacs here, all the lilacs on the island, all the lilacs in the world. I become a huge hollow tube, an empty funnel for the purple lilac love to pour itself into. It pours and I swallow, feeling firsthand the joy that flows between the river and its banks, the sea and its shore.

I am lost in the current, my awareness of self swept away. Something is filled, sated in the exchange. An overwhelming sense of peace is present.

I come to, find myself back among the flowers. I watch as my own hand reaches for a stem.

May I pick you, I ask. Of course, the reply. My fingers choose a great big flower head, fully a foot long, bending the stem until it snaps. I cringe, but the flower just smiles.

I close my eyes, brushing the blossoms gently across my face. I stroke my cheek, nose, brow. My skin tingles. I feel a soft subtle energy running through me. I grow more playful, brushing my arms, legs, chest.

I start dancing, an elfish grin on my face. I tap and pat, jump and twirl. Good thing this place is fairly deserted, I think, seeing myself as quite a spectacle to human eyes. Not so to us, I hear, feeling the playful presence of nature spirits.

I end up with my clothes in the bushes, prancing around with the lilac and other devas. Together we sing creation's praise, bringing great joy and gratitude to the simple beauty of flowers. Images of elves and fairies come alive, and we celebrate life and each other with much delight. Spring is ushered in for me this day, along with my part in it.

Bahamian Watsu

It was midweek and the trip was going great. Everyone was relaxed, people were being really open and honest with each other. We'd had some pretty powerful encounters with the dolphins, and our group energy was high.

We were snorkeling an old boat wreck, a big hollow hull in about eight feet of water. The thousands of fish that take refuge there were amazing to watch, pouring themselves up, over and around the larger jack fish as he swam through the middle of them. I was completely absorbed in their fluidity, these fish a silver cloud that moved so gracefully.

Just then Debbie splashed up to me, a mischievous look on her face. "It's time," she said, pulling off her bathing suit and splashing back to join the others.

Every once in a while nudity has a way of showing up on our trips. It's usually initiated by someone with the firsthand experience of being in the ocean as naked as the fish.

Being bare in the water is a most incredible sensation. Just try taking a bath with your clothes on. I'd forgotten the pleasures of nude bathing a long time ago. I think by age three I was stuffed in a way-too-tight hand me down pair of swim trunks, and was doomed to spend the rest of my aquatic experiences clothed if it wasn't for my summer as a camp counselor. I worked for a camp that had 'The Fifth Freedom,' the freedom to swim with or without clothes. Taking off my clothes in front of the other camp counselors was a bit scary at first, but by the second or third swim I got over my shyness. With that behind me, I began to notice something extraordinary—swimming in the water without any clothes felt absolutely incredible!

Without the drag of a swimsuit, my body moved easily through the water. And the lake—it touched me in ways I'd forgotten since childhood. I felt free and open, a wonderful sense of exposure. I had nothing to hide! The sensation of my unclothed body moving through the water communicated a feeling of warmth, fullness and well being.

Since then, given the right time and place, I'll readily swim in the buff. I still feel shy when my clothes first come off, but I know it'll pass, allowing me to feel once again the ocean's amniotic bliss.

But nudity's a touchy issue with a lot of people. So I don't usually bring it up. If it does come up, I let the group handle it. It's another one of those things I learned to let go of. I found it has a way of working itself out.

Which it was this day. Now that suits were coming off, I was ready to join the buff bunnies. I had on a T-shirt and trunks. The T-shirt was to cover my back, already red from a full day in the hot Bahamian sun. I slipped off my shorts and joined in a spontaneous splash fight.

After awhile, I wanted some quiet time to just float in the waves, so I swam down the beach for some privacy.

There was barely any surf. The waves were gentle, just a few inches high, breaking right on the sand where the water was warmest. I lay down at the water's edge.

I was face up, my feet floating open to the waves, head resting on sand. The waves rolled gently in, rocking my body easily, rhythmically. I felt like the tail of a whale as it undulated through the deep.

My T-shirt ballooned up, flush with the waters of each incoming gush, draping itself back down, cool and enticing, as each wave receded. It was a wet, rhythmical massage, and I relaxed fully into it.

I was half laying, half floating. My awareness began to drift and expand. I felt the hairs on my body rocking back and forth with the rhythm of the waves. I became alive and entranced.

The water moved me, touched me, rocked me. It embraced me with the tenderness of a lover. I felt the whole ocean playing with me in her mouth, sucking me in and sliding me out. Her waters mixed easily with my own salty tears.

The ocean, the water, the waves; the sun and sand and I, we became one, holding and being held in a gentle rocking comfort. It was a profoundly intimate experience, one that brought me deep inside myself. So much so that I became self conscious. I opened my eyes to take a quick look down the beach, to make sure I wasn't attracting any attention, feeling shy and vulnerable in my openness. No one was looking my way, they were busy and about their own play.

I closed my eyes and gave myself back to the water. I felt the whole ocean, all seven seas, vibrantly alive and directing this encounter. She, this vast and hugely feminine water, was running the show, and I had the good grace to surrender to her.

She became a liquid, light-filled goddess; loving, embracing and absorbing all that lives within her with total equanimity. Through her, I became aware of all the fish, all the mammals, all the plants and microbes living within her. I felt the incredible joy and rapture of the sea and everything in it. I'd no idea how ecstatic it was to be a part of her world.

She rocked me and rocked me. My heart swelled to bursting, I feared I'd explode from so great a love. The intimacy of our encounter brought more tears, and with it came shame, the shame of receiving something so wonderful. Who was I, to be the lover of oceans? Who was I, to think myself worthy of this grace? The pain of this shame grew, until it separated us. Again and again I'd pull away, taking myself from her embrace.

Propping myself up on an elbow, I'd look pensively down the beach at my friends, afraid still of any unwanted attention I might have attracted. I was blaming them for the source of my discomfort, a way to dodge the truth of my own unworthiness.

Just as soon as shame would have me pull myself from the water, I'd be filled with an overwhelming longing for her. Grief would assail me for breaking with so great a love, until, first with fear and then with relief, I'd lay myself back down into her embrace.

Every time I lay back down, she was there to receive me. It was as if I'd never left. My pain and confusion would slip easily away.

After awhile, my discomfort lessened. I found myself sinking deeper and deeper into her embrace. Her gentle acceptance moved me deeply, helped me let go a longtime grip to the feelings of unworthiness, an unworthiness I never knew I had.

I softened, leaving behind more and more as I sank. I no longer saw myself as a man in the water with the ocean. My identity became fluid, I felt myself man to woman, masculine to feminine. Over time this too washed away, and I felt my feminine essence rising up to meet her, stirred and awakened by her touch.

Never before have I known the ocean as such. She has become a living entity, an essence of great love and acceptance. There are times I return to play in her arms, aware of her loving embrace. Other times I grasp to feel her, and come up with only a memory. But even then I know she is there, and it's only I, in my small vision of self, that pretends not to see her. I'm comforted in this remembering, knowing she's alive and well, blessing the waters that flow through the very veins and cells of my body.

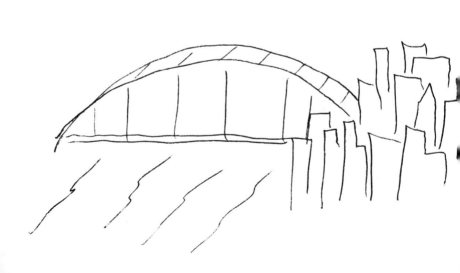

Eyes of the Beholder

I was in New York City to do some consulting work for a client. I had arrived the night before, to get a full night's sleep. The hotels I usually go to were full, so I had a travel agent find a room for me.

I arrive in the dark. The cab pulls up to the curb and I look out. The first thing I see is a porn shop. Then another. Tucked up out of the way between the two is a dingy little sign, 'Hotel.' My hotel.

My stomach sinks. I start reviewing my options. It's late, I'm tired, there's little chance I'll find another. What the hey, it can't be all that bad. The cabbie gives me an encouraging tip, "It's not a really bad neighborhood, just don't go out at night." It's after 10 p.m.

I unload my bags and walk in. The manager is friendly, upbeat. He's watching "The Shining" on TV, a show I've never watched (on purpose). I get my key and start walking the two flights up to my room.

I'm hypersensitive, all eyes and ears. Is this place okay, is it safe? It's old, dirty and a bit funky, but it doesn't seem dangerous. I find my room, unlock the door and step in. It's tiny, all I smell is stale smoke, and the carpet's full of burn marks. Yeow, I wonder if they rent this room by the hour.

I check the sheets; they look clean. I sit down, tired and unsure. The air's so dead I can hardly breathe, so I go back down and ask for another room. He gives me another key. I walk in, guarded. The air's stale, but free of smoke. The burns on the carpet are no longer a surprise. There's a window, I can always get some fresh air. And the sheets look clean. What the hey, I say, and unpack.

Later, after I've slipped off my shoes (I'm still not ready to go barefoot), I open my little window to bring in some cool autumn air. The window looks out into a dark, dusty air vent that's chock full of trash. It's stultifying, there's not a drop of oxygen out there.

Groaning, I shut it and lay down, depressed. I don't trust the air, I don't trust the carpet, I don't want to touch the bathroom tiles or the sink or the shower. I feel like a petri dish in a sea of germs, all waiting to jump aboard and start growing.

I start chuckling. What a predicament! I've stayed in a lot worse. After getting ready for bed, I crawl under the sheets.

As I lay there, ready for sleep, I realize I'm still tense. My body's rigid and my lungs are taking tiny sips of air. I'm holding my energy in, wrapping my aura tightly around me. I'll never get any rest this way. There's nothing I can do to change what's around me; it's clear my work is on the inside.

So I start chanting and blessing the place, inviting Guadeloupe and all the saints and siddhas to join me. As I lay there, listening to the names of the divine roll off my tongue, I remember that the sheets that cover me are from the flowers of cotton plants, grown in the deep red earth under a warm southern sky. I imagine the shakti of the sun as it courses through these threads. The image comes to life, the sheets start to glow, and I find myself in a cocoon of light. Memories of the divine become real; I feel myself surrounded by angelic beings. The wooden frame of the bed becomes alive, grows branches, sprouts leaves, and I fall asleep in a forest of God's creation.

I awake refreshed, as if in a temple. Sleepily I look around, remembering where I am. The room looks different now. Cheerfully I go off to work and return later that night, to peep show row, to crawl into my hermitage of light. The siddhas, saints and devas are there waiting for me.

Winter's Call

Recently we moved to a small barrier island on the coast of New England. It's a beautiful spot, full of sand, wind and water. This end of the island's packed with old summer cottages that are daily turning into three-story homes. I love our street, it's full of kids our son plays with, and I know everyone here by name. But at night, when I go for a walk, it's south, to the unlit part of the beach, that I head. Here the night sky is dazzling, and out from the depths of the Atlantic springs forth wave after wave of water to break upon the sand at my feet.

I love this walk at night, especially in a winter's storm. I start out reluctant, a part of me preferring the warmth and comfort of home. But the storm's pull is strong, rattling the windows, howling at the door. Its invitation is irresistible, and finally I go. By the time I walk the block and a half to the beach, I'm smiling.

My cheeks cool quickly, and the warmth I've carried from home leaks out with each step, each swing of my arms. I know if I meander too slowly, I'll be cold and shivering in minutes. To stay out here I must light the fire of my own body, so I walk fast, straight into the wind.

Soon I'm breathing heavy, sucking in lungfulls of frozen air. All the thoughts of the day are left behind with my footprints, swallowed by the night. The core of my body heats up, pumps fiery hot blood to my arms and legs, fingers and toes. The sting of the wind softens, and my cheeks grow warm, melting the windblown snow on my face. It trickles down my neck and onto my chest, bringing shivers, mixing with my own sweat, until it disappears into the warmth of my body. My heart swells and my head swoons. Yee-ha! I'm happy to be alive.

I feel myself surrounded by holy spirits; devas, fairies and angels who sing praise with me in the shrieking of the wind. I reach out to them, arms upraised. My steps lighten and I twirl, pulling them into me, pouring myself into them, into the storm. We blend together, merging in the night, and the beach becomes the vastness of the Milky Way, we the stars upon its shore. Together we dance, across galaxies filled with light.

I stumble home, drunk with the ecstasy of union. Soon I'm between the cool sheets of bed, listening to the storm outside, feeling it raging within. I'm kin with all the creatures out there, the deer and coyotes, rabbits and birds, all curled up in their nests. I pull the covers close, drifting to sleep.

Baby Beach Buddha

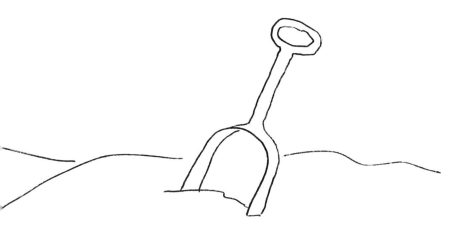

I was running down the beach, enjoying the warm Hawaiian sun. The beach was narrow, and I wove my way between trees and coral. I loved this spot, an undeveloped strip of shore between my hotel and the next. It was raw and pristine, and I welcomed the occasional piece of trash, left alone in this unmanicured refuge. I let my energy reach out to the wildness around me, embracing the undulating groves of trees shaped by the wind and weather.

I was here as a part of a conference, my job to help people connect more deeply with Nature. They were ready for it after a day indoors. We'd already spent an afternoon playing on this narrow strip of land, burying each other in the sand, splashing together in the waves. I was out recharging my own batteries, playing around with some ideas for our next adventure.

The refuge ended. I came out onto a crowded public beach. I reeled my senses in from their reverie, looking out for the many moving bodies crossing my path. It was an abrupt change, like driving from the Midwest into Manhattan.

I liked this beach, it had a lot of families. A couple of kids were playing at the water's edge, letting the gentle surf roll them around, taking a ride in the world's biggest washing machine. How easily they surrendered to its play. Others were playing the age-old game of wave tag. They'd run down after a retreating wave, right to the water's edge, then scoot back up just out of reach of the next, yelling and screaming the whole time. They were having a blast.

I continued running, and then something caught the corner of my eye. I turned and saw a toddler, naked except for a diaper. He held a small plastic shovel in his hand. It was full of sand, and he was pouring it onto his leg. Something about the deliberateness of his actions grabbed me.

I stopped running, looked closer. He continued pouring, his face rapt with attention.

His eyes, his gaze, his entire essence was drinking in his actions. Complete one-mindedness, so complete it pulled me in with it. I stood mesmerized as the sand continued to slowly pour from the lip of the shovel and down, down, down onto his leg.

He was riveted. His focus gathered my own. I saw the shovel become the sand, and the sand become his leg. It was like watching a Genie come out of a bottle. I felt one with him, became a part of him, looked out his eyes.

The sand continued to fall. He was drinking it all in, feeling the movement of muscles, tendons and tissues sliding around each other, movements he was just now mastering, sensations that brought great joy and pleasure.

I watched as he mastered the art of pouring, and as he poured, the shovel becoming a part of him. I felt the sand touching his skin, releasing its warmth into his leg. I watched as the sand became the beach, and he along with it.

Quantum physicists and sages of old tell us that the world around us is a part of us, that there are no definite boundaries between me and thee, that we are all one. They say that the lines we have drawn are random and illusory in nature. Watching this baby buddha, I remembered the truth of these words, felt the power of our oneness.

And the look. I saw God looking out at his creation, marveling at the magic and wonder of it all. I saw God enjoying life through the eyes of this child.

I heard a voice, the voice I love that I hear so clearly in Nature. It told me to be still and to drink deeply. Even now I feel the warm sand cascading gently onto my leg, feel my leg become a part of the beach, the beach become the shore.

Part 2

Poetry & Praise

Late Night Storm

Doors banging
shades clacking
palm trees
bent and bobbing

Winds howling
night sky flashing–
storm's long ethereal arm
reaching inside and tugging,
lifting sheets and sleep from me

Staccato bursts
of pelting rain
run rampant
across rooftops,
A large restless dragon
roams free tonight

Earth's cracked lips
soften,
the falling rain moistens
her parched throat

Wetness oiling
internal organs,
she begins
a long slow swallow–
Water pooling
in the tiny small ripples
of her smile

Cisterns filling
after months of dryness,
people smiling
in their sleep
Dreams of wetness
shaking loose
hardened crusts
Weeks of tensions
and squabbles
melt and dissolve

The palms
bob and weave with ease
Tensions lifted,
flow restored

Goosebumps
race across this body
little electric storms of excitement,
puckish atoms dancing,
bouncing across skin
I am a harp,
the wind and rain
play me
Somewhere inside,
strings quiver
in response

Storm leaving
night softening
dark settling,
everything quieting
Refreshed,
I snuggle deeper
plunge back into dreaming, smiling
a wetness blessing

Somewhere Among the Flowers

That's where you'll find him
tucked cozily
beneath their canopy

It's his safe haven
among friends
gentle enough to listen

These flowers,
his guardians
warding off
all judgement
Weaving
a web of enchantment
as they sway in the breeze

It's where
I found him
after many years of searching
Here, among those
as gentle as he

At first,
I never thought to look
in such a fairy nest
Then,
I was too afraid,
ashamed to be caught
with head in flower bed

In truth
I found him
quite by accident

It was a time
when I sought refuge of my own,
and was drawn, called
to get down on hands and knees
and crawl in
amongst the petals and leaves

Here was another kingdom
magical, beyond compare

The flowers spoke to me
soothing, softly
touching an ancient place

within me
My heart sang
its own reply

It was here
I found him,
this gentle child, keeper of tenderness

Maybe in truth
I'm part elemental–
the magic of their kingdom
calls me so

Maybe, as a child
I fell asleep
inside a pagan circle
full of garlands and lilies
its edges spun
with prayers and blessings
from those light of feather
and foot

Perhaps
it's just my nature
to love these flowers so

I remember
seeing magic stirring
beneath the low lying branches
and under the crowns
of daisies

Many were the wishes
and prayers I sang,
joining in
the magic and the fun

It was here
I left him
to join the ranks
of a frantic race

It's here
I rejoin him
leaving behind
my own trail of tears

It's now
from the peace of this place
I tell this tale
of joyful reunion

The dance continues,
the magic stirs—
all is
as it was before

It's as if
I never left
Maybe
it was all just a dream
I pinch myself, smiling

Sledding

It's been a dry winter
with very little snow
Our six year old
cries when it melts

Yesterday
it started snowing
and left a dusting, maybe two inches
on the ground by nightfall

Quickly we grabbed our sleds
and headed for the hills

The park was empty
except for the tracks
of toboggans and footsteps

Up we climb
slipping and sliding
to the top, to survey
the landscape below

"I'm going first"
he yells, as he plops
on his sled and is off–
another set of tracks
down the hill

I smile at the sight–
a child
rocketing downhill
at warp speed
I imagine the grin
on his face
is as big as mine

In my hand
I hold the remnants
of a tattered toy
This purple plastic sled
my ticket
to freedom

With a hoot and a holler
I mount my mighty steed
a push and a shove
and I too
am flying

I yell with abandon,
delight and trepidation
and arrive at the bottom
intact, one piece

He
has already started up
little legs
pumping and churning,
intent
on another thrill

I gingerly stand
and check my back
the over-40
reconnaissance
of the body

A few more runs
and I too
am heading
back up the hill
as fast as he

Drunk Again!

Drunk again,
oh no!
I should've known better
I stayed too long
in your golden fields
and along your autumn crest

A short walk
was all I planned–
A quick respite
from a harried day

Ten minutes, maybe an hour
has turned into a sunset, a moonrise
and an evening so enchanting
my feet won't move

On, I plead
Onward to home!
I will be late,
the park is closed!
We must depart

now, while there's light enough
to find our way home

You are, the reply
Are what? I ask
Home, you answer
and every cell in my body
tingles in response

I feel caught,
trapped
between a world I love,
a world that understands, accepts, loves
and nurtures me completely,
a world in which there is no time
where everything just is,

and a world that says come on,
you're late
you have to leave before
they lock the gate.

So here I stand
so drunk
from the sky

the stars
and the evening's breeze
I cannot move

Part 3

Body
Wisdom

The body always tells the truth ~
Just try hiding a blush

Nipples

I took a walk on the refuge last night. It was just after sunset, the sky to the west was gray, threatening rain. I walked along the narrow tar road, bordered by marsh and shrubs. The place was alive with birds, squawking, flying, swooping and singing. It's nesting season, they're busy setting up house.

I love to watch them flit from one side of the road to the other. Some with bugs in their beaks, others with little twists of grass. Some fly up close to check me out, singing loudly, waiting for my reply. I chirped out my best, my own chest filled with the joy of the season.

I stopped in front of a hedge, a mix of wild roses and other plants. I know this place well, there's roses here that are an extra rich red. Some days I'll pick one to carry with me, and after breathing in its fragrance, I'll rub it over my face, brushing away any tensions from the day.

I've come to love this spot with its mix of sights and sounds. It's full of surprises. All I have to do is stop and watch for a few minutes, and I'll discover something new. This time I noticed a small tree with shiny olive green leaves out in the middle. It had little pointed spikes of bright white flowers. I could smell them from the road, a sharp, sweet smell.

A deep gray bird with a beak full of straw flew from across the street and landed in the bushes. He turned and looked at me. I felt completely at peace, and sensed he did as well. I smiled as we enjoyed each other's affection. "What a wonderful place to live!" I said out loud, surprising myself. He sang his agreement.

I felt him welcoming me to share this hedge, with the myriad of other creatures, as my own home. I accepted, and he disappeared into its thickness. This hedge housed a wonderful community, of which I was now a member. My heart opened, and I felt my essence pour itself out and mix with the pool of plant, animal and spirit energies that live here.

After awhile I continued walking, feeling expansive and open. My thoughts moved quietly around me, there was a softness to my being. The dark clouds on the horizon were closer, and a cold wind kicked its way across the marsh, pushing itself up against me. My skin rippled with the touch of its coolness, and I felt my nipples tingle from under my shirt. The tingling felt great, a waking up of my senses, plugging me into the energy of the wind, the marsh, the oncoming storm. Yet the tingling brought with it a bittersweet feeling. What's this? I wondered, and as I pondered this question, a memory flashed before me.

I was about 12 years old. Some of the kids in my neighborhood were already growing hair on their bodies. Billy, a full two years younger than I, would proudly show anyone who'd look his latest discovery, three dark curly hairs poking out from his armpit. I made fun of his display and teased him for his excitement, at the same time hiding my own envy. Every time I'd go to the bathroom I'd check my armpits in the mirror and pull my underwear down, searching for the start of my own fur patch, my personal badge of manhood. But all that stared back at me was the soft pink skin of boyhood.

Over time, I got scared. I was afraid something was wrong with me, became fearful that puberty might pass me by. I'd read about such a thing, knew it was possible. And then, to make matters worse, my nipples started to ache. They really hurt. I had to be careful putting my shirts on and off, something I'd never done before. Until then, I'd never really thought much about nipples, they were for girls. But my chest's sudden call for attention petrified me. What was going on? No one had ever said anything about this. Was everything okay, or was something weird happening? And then it hit me, the most dreaded thought I could've imagined. What if, through some cruel trick of nature, I was growing breasts instead of hair?

This thought utterly terrified me. It haunted me day and night. Even now it's hard to communicate the depths of that fear. It was the fear of being a freak; half male, half female, stuck permanently between two worlds. I was already afraid I might not be male enough, having learned from my dad that I wasn't tough enough, strong enough, mean enough. I remember him being angry at me for my love of

nature. I had tried hard to be tougher, put away anything that might be remotely childish, and learned to
walk with a swagger. I was terrified he was right, and
now I was filled with shame from images of my chest
swelling with breasts.

I remember how this episode ended. After weeks
of agony, I steeled myself into action. Through sheer
act of will, with a hardness I had learned to mimic, I
slammed the door on my body. I turned my back on
its sensations. I cursed it, sent it away, and told it I
would only acknowledge it when it brought me the
maleness I so desperately sought. I remember thinking that this was the right way to behave, the manly
way to deal with the situation. I was so afraid my
body might be feminine, I would have rather it died
than sprout breasts. For it to have done so would
have been the ultimate act of betrayal. And so I
shut out its messages, of both pain and pleasure.

This all came back to me last night, as the air danced
sweetly around me. I felt my nipples awakening, a
mix of pleasure and pain rippling through them. I
felt the fears, the judgements and the shame of my

past at the same time I felt the tingling of their present pleasure. And I said yes to it, yes to it all. There, in the gathering night, the wind playing across my chest, my body alive with the pleasure of it, I said yes.

I took back into myself the child who was so attuned to the forces of nature, who so loved intimacy with the world around him. I accepted fully the pains and the pleasures of his body, his life. I continued walking into the night and into the coming rain, feeling vibrantly alive as the falling waters soaked thru my windbreaker, kissing my skin with its wetness. I laughed as it poured and became pelting, soaking me quickly, leaving me shivering.

I ran back to the parking lot, smiling sweetly at the memory of my insecurities. I felt full, whole, a complete love and acceptance of this part of me. I knew that this was a part of me my father was afraid of, ashamed of, a part of himself he dared not trust. And it was alright. For I am grateful, ever so grateful, to be reunited with the feminine part of life and the wonderful receptivity she brings.

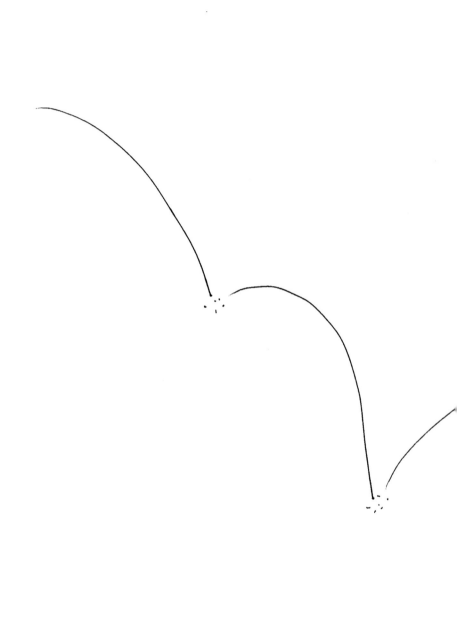

Wolfish Friend

I want to tell you about a new friend of mine. I have to be careful as I write, as he's sitting right beside me. (He's now under my arm—oh God, he just jumped onto my lap!)

He's a wolf spider. I use the term "he" loosely. He's gray, black and white, has eight legs (that's how I know he's a spider), and he's climbing up my shirt, with an occasional pause to look at me with his multiple eyes. (He just disappeared under my shirt!)

I first saw him a week ago, walking across my desk. Stalking, really. Moving each leg slowly, pausing, looking around, moving some more. His deliberateness caught my attention, and I put a piece of paper down in front of him. He stepped boldly onto it, and I lifted him up onto the feather that sits atop my computer (I just felt him jump from my shirt collar onto my neck!)

Once upon a time, it wasn't possible for me to be friends with a spider. I was afraid of their bite. I was afraid of being bitten by a lot of things, and spiders and bugs were high on the list, right up there with our neighbor's bulldog. The phrase, "There's a bug on you!" was enough to make my skin crawl. (He just leapt from my neck onto my left arm—what a hop!)

I'd always been fascinated by bugs as a kid. They came in so many shapes and sizes. But I was never on close terms with them. I always assumed they'd bite, pinch, drill or spray the first chance they got. That's what I'd have done, if I'd been picked up by something a gazillion times bigger than me.

I grew up on an old farm, and sometimes during summer we'd run through the tall grass with a big old metal bucket. We'd drag it open-mouthed behind us, running big crazy loops through patches of milkweed and purple vetch. We'd finish our tirade at the top of the hill, back where we started, and plunk ourselves down, panting, to inspect our catch.

It never failed. Inside that bucket was a circus of bugs, the whole thing boiling with action. I learned to look from arm's length, at least until all the grasshoppers made their rapid escape. It was just like a cowboy shoot-out, the way those hoppers would come flying out of the pail. When things quieted down, we'd peer closer at the thick mat of insects crawling dizzily on the bucket's bottom.

Bugs were cool. I had no doubt about that. But still I kept my distance.

Once, when I was around 10, I was doing my bucket brigade, running full-tilt boogie through the fields below the apple trees. Something caught my eye, and I stopped short. There, right in front of me, was a HUGE spider's web. It stretched easily four feet across. My skin started to crawl. Then, horror of horrors, I saw a great big fat spider sitting right in the middle of it, inches from my face. I got the willies, and turned to make my exit.

I took a step to the right and...stopped. Oh God, another web, right in my path. Whew, I almost walked into him too!

I turned the other way and—froze. A third web, complete with spider, right in front of me. I held rigid, and slowly it dawned on me that not only was I was right smack in the middle of a patch of spiders, there was a good chance one of them was already crawling on me!

I don't remember how I got back to the top of the hill, but I imagine it was pretty quick.

After awhile I calmed down. There were no spiders on me (that I knew of), and I didn't break out in any large welts. Curiosity got the better of me, and I carefully retraced my steps back to the spider's den for a closer look.

I felt a mix of awe and revolt as I looked at them. They were big, much bigger than I wanted to mess with. They were black, white and yellow, had very long legs, and moved a little too fast for my comfort.

Over time, I got used to them. They were cool to watch, and I learned that they hung out on the outer edge of their webs and only came out when they'd caught something or were disturbed. I found that if I shook their web, they'd run out into the middle and bounce the whole thing up and down like a trampoline. Their way of saying "Buzz off," I guess.

It wasn't long before I caught a grasshopper and threw him in. I wanted to watch these guys in action. Man, those spiders were fast. Before the hopper could kick himself free, that spider'd be out there doing a spinning jig over him so fast, he was mummified in seconds.

My fascination grew, and I ended up carrying some spiders (in a very big jar, with very thick glass) up the hill and onto the thorn bushes behind our house. I placed them about two feet apart, and by the end of the summer, had a whole row running the full length of the hedge. I'd catch grasshoppers, big green and brown ones, throw them into the web and watch those spiders spin. I felt bad about my role in the demise of so many grasshoppers, but figured hey, these guys got to eat, they'd have eaten where they were, and since I moved them up here, it was my job to feed them.

That's been my history with spiders. I loved them from afar, and I never ever let them crawl on me. Until today, when my wolfish friend (where did he go?) crawled over a mound of papers and over to my keyboard. He then sat there and watched me for over an hour. He finally advanced closer, out into the open, between the keyboard and the table's edge, inches from my elbow. There he stopped and looked up at me. I looked back, sent him a welcome with my thoughts, and felt a very friendly hello coming back. This was cool, so I put aside my papers and gave him my full attention.

I beheld quite a royal creature. His stance was strong and sturdy, his body was covered with tiny hairs. I admired how he held his ground in the face of a creature so much bigger than him. I sent him my admiration and blessings.

I wanted to go further, fully explore this marvelous creature, so I put my finger on the table in front of him. It was a bold move, and we both paused. Then he ever so casually stepped onto it. I felt a tingling where he touched me, tiny footsteps across my hand.

He paused and raised his head. I looked with wonder down into his many eyes, curious what he was thinking. I admired the courage that allowed him to assess me as calmly as I assessed him. I very clearly felt his acknowledgement of my respect, a quiet knowing from within me. It surprised me, this gentle knowing, and I realized with delight how calm and peaceful I felt. He advanced further, walking along my forearm. I had the sense that he was having fun as he picked his way across and over the hairs on my arm. I sure was.

Somewhere in the background I heard a voice say, "Hey, I have a spider on my arm and shouldn't I be careful?" It was then I realized I was unafraid of being bit. Sure, he had a couple of rather hairy things that looked like fangs hanging below his eyes, but all I felt was mutual respect coming from him. How cool. My heart swelled.

I've gotten so carried away with this story that I've lost track of him. Given his determination, I imagine he's sitting atop my head right now, enjoying a bird's eye view of the room. I move mindfully, delighting in my carefulness, another demonstration of my admiration. I imagine he appreciates it.

Sequoias to the Rescue

It was a crazy time. I was between careers, running around anxious and exhausted, worried about paying the bills. My body was tense, I had the coffee jitters, (even though I don't drink coffee) and my heart was racing. I was miserable and calling for help.

I got no reply. I felt alone, isolated. I breathed, I walked, I prayed; I meditated and I chanted. I did everything I knew to invoke the divine. I sat and felt —anxious. I sat some more, felt some more, got stir crazy. Whatever was going on was stuck to me like gum, so I got up and threw myself into the myriad of chores clamoring for attention.

And then it happened. I was busy cleaning out the lint trap in the clothes dryer when a wave of energy moved into me. It simply stepped inside me, like I was a car and it the driver. It was a powerful presence; tall, wide, deep and strong. It was just suddenly there, filling me with its peace. I found myself held in a gentle, comforting strength that loved me deeply. My shoulders relaxed, my face softened and my breathing slowed. I can feel the softening, even now.

My body trusted this energy completely, sank right into it. My mind was startled, surprised at the suddenness of this appearance as well as my body's complete surrender to it. My very cells were fully in tune with this energy, and I didn't know who or what it was!

So I sat down, closed my eyes and looked inside. I tuned into the incredible hugeness of this energy. It felt like a collective group of beings. And then I saw their shape — trees. Sequoias. Huge, tall, old and wise. I have sat beneath them many times, have laughed, cried and camped beneath them, but it never felt like this. It was mind boggling to have them come here, to me, thousands of miles away. My body continued to relax, drinking in their care, as a tremendous amount of gratitude welled up within me.

They held me gently, and as I rested in their embrace, I saw these giants as angels who choose trees as a way to express their essence. I saw them as ancient, gentle and loving beings, incarnating in the form of sequoias and redwoods as a way to give permanence to their physicality. I saw how they work as conduits between the stars and our planet, receiving all kinds of spinning celestial energies from the heavens, channeling them through their physicality, grounding them into our earth. I no longer saw them as trees with spirits; they became spirits who've taken on the form of trees. I saw how they work as a group, traversing the planet in energetic form, going to different hot spots to share their grounding influence.

The size of their energy was huge. It went up hundreds of miles into the sky, tremendously beneficent tornadoes bringing all kinds of powerful energies deep into our planet's core. And then I saw the precariousness of their physicality. We are weakening their connection to the earth through our cutting of them. They provide a vital service, acupuncture needles in the hot growing spine of our Pacific, balancing and harmonizing many forms of elemental energy.

I know if we cut them all down, they'd still remain in spirit, doing their healing work as best they can. But being in physical form gives them the ability to transmute and harmonize these energies in a very powerful and direct way.

I felt scared at the fragileness of their fate, unable to run from our lumber hunger. An age-old fear, the terror of the loss of Nature, struck me deep in my heart. It was the terror of being left on a dead, sterile planet, a planet devoid of green growing things. This fear shook me, rattled me, overwhelmed me. Once again I was lost in a sea of despair. And then, somehow, they removed it. They took this fear from me as though it were the tiniest of splinters. Just like that, the huge hole in my heart was gone. I was again filled with the wonderful peace of their presence. Wow, I was in awe.

I need to tell your story, I thought, ready to jump up and write. Relax, they said, we're not here to get help. We're here to give healing, and give they did. After months of tensions and worries, the dry and cracked parts of me soaked up their nurturing. I was the plant and they the gardeners, gentle and loving in their care.

I'm sitting in a little hollow, a gully amidst a sea of sand dunes. It's filled with short stubby pines whose tops reach as high as the dunes that surround us.

The gusty March wind is racing crazily through their tops, making a soft swishing sound, like someone sweeping, or the singing of a lullaby.

I just finished a long walk on the beach, and I'm sitting in here to get out of the wind. I'm chilled to the bone, ready for warmer weather. Winter's on retreat, but today the wind carries another blast of its arctic frigidness, reminding all it hasn't left just yet.

The sun breaks through the clouds, blessing me with its warmth. Each splash of light's a love letter from Spring, heralding her imminent return. It's cozy in here, all's still, my refuge from the cold.

Clouds cover the sun, the temperature drops. The wind kicks up, finds me down here among the trees. It rushes down my collar, pouring a frigid wave across my back.

My body reacts—goosebumps ripple through me, sweep across my skin like a rainsquall across the prairie. My habit is to tighten, pulling in muscles to conserve heat. But today I relax. Perhaps because the wind is my friend, I stay open, and ride the wave as it races across me.

I become a living landscape and it the rider, a wild horse running free. Rouge hordes of shivers mark its travels, racing and turning, a joyful wave rolling. It surprises me, running zigzag down my arms and into my armpits. It tickles!

The clouds part and the sun pops back out, its bright rays blasting down, bathing me in light. Its warmth is instant, hungrily my face soaks it in.

I bask, a lizard on a rock, heat rays penetrating. I soften and settle, inviting it deeper, bones warming after a long winter.

Soon I'm hot. My face is flush and my armpits are sweating. I open my collar, inviting the wind back in. I'm ready for another rollercoaster ride through the vastness of the prairie.

Dolphin Dream
Embracing the Matriarch

I'm walking along the main drag of an old tourist town. The road runs alongside the beach, the water's a few feet away. The sun's just set, night is falling. There's a lot of people walking around, enjoying the evening.

Suddenly a pod of dolphins start jumping out of the water, barely 30 feet from shore. Seeing them's a total shock to my system. I hear other people's surprised reactions, gasps and sighs. The pod, maybe 15 in number, swims closer to shore. Something pulls me to them, and I run to the water's edge to greet them.

To my surprise, they swim closer. They're in barely 3 feet of water. I'm irresistibly drawn to them. Without thinking, I rush in. I'm shocked to find myself naked, my swimsuit in hand. A part of me is trying to put the suit on as I hurry to greet my friends, but I let it

go, and it disappears in the water, along with any
worries about my nudity in this most public place.

There is one dolphin who comes in the closest to
greet me. I feel an overwhelming connection with
her. I fall into the water, wrapping my arms around
her wet, sensual body. Her skin is slippery, her body
warm and firm. A wonderful sense of relief floods
me, my cells tingle with delight and recognition.

She's the leader of this pod, the matriarch. But she's
the most intimate of friends to me. The breadth of
our camaraderie runs deep, into depths that bring up
shame in my humanness. But I hang on, refusing to
break the connection with so vital a force. She is not
as mother to me, but partner. Not in the sense of
human relationship, with all it's expectations and sin-
gularity. No, this is different, and I feel places within
me healing as we hold each other. Places so deep, tears
so old, I'm aware of the ancientness of our existence.

We arc not human and dolphin, we are two souls
from the same soul family, uniting after a long and
arduous journey. She has come here to affirm a part

of self I've sought, prayed and yearned for but dared not believe existed. I'm overcome with love and gratitude, getting back a part of myself.

She starts clicking to me through her blow hole. She sings me songs, songs of the sea and of childhood. They're familiar, from another place a long time ago, long before I took a human path and she a dolphin. A part of me struggles to remember, to learn the words, while another part of me is happy to just listen and be sung to. Like a contented child I relax fully into her, letting the song and its images carry me. Songs of the sea, simple and beautiful, as life is meant to be.

As we lay there in embrace, the shame returns, washing me in its red flush of embarrassment. It shows me a picture of a man, lying naked in the surf, with his arms around a dolphin like it's his long lost friend. But the love that's flowing between us is too powerful, and the shame finds no hold, no place to stick. It ebbs and flows through me with the waves, washing me clean, losing itself in the vastness of the water.

I surrender my identity as human, the illusion of individuality dissolving in our intimacy. I lovingly stroke her body, feeling the calluses and scars of her journey.

Then it's as if I'm back in the world of mankind. I'm aware of people around us. "We must help these beached dolphins," someone says. I'm shocked to hear such an interpretation of this sacred event, helpless dolphins stranded on the shore. But it's as if the tide has run out, and I'm on the sand with my soul sister. I'm confused, slipping into the human view of the event, become concerned. Are they okay? Is something wrong? It does seem strange for her to be almost completely out of the water.

But the solution is simple; a dropoff into deeper water is right beside us. Someone instructs me to carry her into the pool, and I struggle whether to go along with this view of things or to stay with my own blissful experience. I choose a middle ground, unwilling to risk my friend's wellbeing, and gently lift her large bulk onto my shoulders and down what has become a stairway into a corridor. I'm shocked at how light her body is, how effortless the carry.

The corridor ends in a subterranean room that's partially flooded. The water's up to my thigh, there's dolphins swimming in it, and people are hurriedly wading around between them. It seems the dolphins and people are working together on something, they're all pretty busy. I feel better, the threat of being beached gone, but I'm confused and feel out of place, wondering what's going on. I ease her into the water and she swims away.

Oh my God, she left! I'm shocked, a lover spurned. Why'd she leave? Where'd she go? I'm in a panic, wondering what to do, when two other dolphins come to my side, nudging for my attention. They see I'm upset, but persistently keep nudging. They want to play. I'm reluctant to switch dance partners so fast, and struggle with what to do.

Inevitably, I turn from my dilemma and touch their noses, those wonderful dolphin snouts that are so playful. They respond by flanking me on my left side, tickling me with their snouts. They want me to lighten up, are working on me so I know everything's okay. They start pushing some reflex on my butt, and I start laughing my head off. They're very deliberate and purposeful in their actions. I laugh and laugh and laugh, and still they push this trigger point. I laugh some more, become self conscious with my outburst. They are persistent, and keep tickling. I laugh out the last of my worries, and wake up laughing.

Conclusion

Thank You!

Thanks for reading these stories. It brings me great pleasure sharing them with you.

When I'm out there, sailing off to the square corners of my known universe, I take you with me. In part for comfort, in part for camaraderie. At other times, for courage. And still others, for someone to share the beauty with, for it's too much for one soul to bear.

How is it that I can experience something so wondrous, I ask. Who am I to receive this grace? Her answer is simple. What is an apple without someone to enjoy its sweetness? What is a flower without anyone to relish its beauty?

When I follow the piper to these riches, I find myself home. Here I know our "purpose," a word only humanity could create. To receive. To enjoy. Simply, wonderfully, that.

May the wonders of Nature inspire us for even more! May our voices rise together in singing her praise!

Planetary Partners~ Bringing Joy to Life!

Birds sing, puppies play,
flowers bloom and sway in the breeze...
waves dance and babies laugh
the invitation is everywhere!

We are born as beacons of joy, and for many of us, some of that joy is lost in the process of 'growing up'. This was certainly true for me. Thankfully, life offers us endless opportunities to join in the fun.

Conferences, Presentations & Spiritual Retreats

I started Planetary Partners with the purpose of bringing more joy into the world. Through talks, dolphin slide shows, playful seminars and retreats, we share in the spirit of fun and adventure. All these programs are audience participatory! For more information about these programs, and to order books and tapes, please visit our website at   **www.PlanetaryPartners.com**

If you don't have web access, you can leave us a message at (978) 499-4960. Because we don't spend much time in the office, the website's the best place to go. It's also loaded with great dolphin photos (in my unbiased opinion).

May you see the light of joy reflected
in the eyes of those around you!

About JoeBaby

JoeBaby's a nature lover from childhood. He grew up in a small town in Maine, climbing trees, going fishing, planting flowers and sleeping outdoors. When he was 20, he moved up north, built a log cabin and lived in the woods for a year.

He's had careers as a carpenter, a healer and a psychotherapist. Currently he consults with Fortune 500 companies, bringing more joy and collaboration to the workplace. He also gives talks, workshops and adventure retreats celebrating the spirit of Joy and receiving the simple grace and beauty of nature.

JoeBaby lives with his wife and son on a small island on the coast of New England. When not going to the beach for a walk or a dip (the waters get mighty chilly this far north…), he's often riding his bike along the marsh, waving his arms, chanting and singing.

Om Shanti!

Recommended Reading

Following are a few of my favorite books…

Conversations with God by Neale Donald Walsch
> Still a bestseller after two years. Yeay America!
> We're waking up!

The Art of Happiness by the Dalai Lama and
Howard Cutler
> I'm awed by The Dalai Lama's constant
> choice for joy and compassion.

Take Time for Your Life by Cheryl Richardson
> If you don't take time for your life, who will?

Autobiography of a Yogi by Paramahansa Yogananda
> I first read this when I was 14. I'm still reading it.

You are That! by Gangaji
> She points ever so clearly and directly to
> the truth of who we are.

The Secret Life of Plants by Peter Thompkins and
Christopher Bird
> This book will rock your boat. Bless your
> dinner, it appreciates it!

The Way of Passion by Andrew Harvey
> An ecstatic portrayal of Rumi. I can't read
> it at night or I'm up 'til dawn.

Emmanuel's Book by Friends of Emmanuel
> For when I forget how truly loved and
> blessed we are.